# The Hungry Hummingbird

# The Hungry Hummingbird

BY APRIL PULLEY SAYRE

ILLUSTRATED BY GAY W. HOLLAND

The Millbrook Press    Brookfield, Connecticut

One bright morning in the heat of August, a young hummingbird flew in search of food.

*Hmmmm*, hummed his wings. He flew to a daisy.

Is this food for hungry hummingbirds?

No! Buzz, buzz! Bees gathered the flower's pollen. But the pollen was fuzzy—not tasty—to the hummingbird's tongue.

He searched again, flying to a yarrow plant.

Is this food for hungry humming-birds?

No! *Flutter, flutter!* Butterflies fed on the flowers. But the hummingbird's tongue couldn't reach much nectar in the tiny blooms.

Feeling hungrier, the humming-bird flew farther. He saw ten tube-shaped flowers. Trumpet vine.

He stuck out his tongue....

Is this food for hungry humming-birds?

Yes! He lapped up one flower's nectar. Then he fed at the other nine.

When he finished those blooms, he couldn't find more.

*Hmmm*, hummed his fast-fanning wings.

Then he spotted some red honey-suckle.

Is this food for hungry humming-birds?

Yes! With his forked tongue, he lapped up the nectar, liquid and sweet.

Red things seemed good. So he tried to find more.

Is this food for hungry humming-birds?

No! *Zoom, zoom!* The car drove off, leaving the hungry bird behind.

Puzzled, the hummingbird searched again.

Is this food for hungry humming-birds?

"No! *Shoo, shoo!* I'm not a flower!" The lady laughed.

The young humming-bird flew on, and spotted something else.

Red sometimes meant food…so the humming-bird followed.

He hovered and watched. This did not look like a flower!

*Tap, tap, tap!* The bird, a sapsucker, tapped a hole in a tree, then licked the tree sap that oozed out.

Could that be food for hungry hummingbirds?

After the sapsucker flew away, the little hummingbird reached out his tongue…and tasted. The sap was sweet and good to eat!

He wanted more. But his tiny bill could not drill holes in trees. Quick! He flew after the sapsucker, sipping sap at the holes it made. But then the bigger bird flew far away.

The young hummingbird was on his own again.

*Hmmmmm....* He zoomed. Close to a swamp. Another hummingbird was feeding at jewelweed flowers. Those flowers weren't red. But they were trumpet shaped....

The little hummingbird swooped down and hovered at the flowers.

Is this food for hungry humming-birds?

Yes!

He fed, then looked for more red flowers—and trumpet-shaped flowers of other colors, too.

Insects often buzzed around the blooms....

*Snap!* He snapped an insect up in his bill.

Is this food for hungry humming-birds?

Yes!

Now the hummingbird had many things to eat: flower nectar, tree sap, and insects. He also saw a gigantic flower, hanging from a hook.

Could this be food for hungry hummingbirds?

Yes! He fed until he was full.

Soon, however, the hummingbird started feeling sleepy. It was getting dark, so he settled on a branch to snooze.

Meanwhile, at the feeder, another hungry young animal was hovering....

Is this food for hungry moths, too?

# The Truth Behind the Story

Young hummingbirds spend a lot of time learning what is good to eat. They try many different shapes and colors of flowers. Eventually, they learn that red flowers usually have lots of sweet nectar. So they check out almost anything that is red.

They have been seen hovering in front of red T-shirts, red hats, and even the brake lights of cars in parking lots! Although young hummingbirds seek out red, orange, or deep pink flowers, they regularly feed from large tubular flowers of other colors, as well.

Nectar is not all they eat. Insects are a major food source, too. Tree sap is an important food for ruby-throated, rufous, ralliope, broad-tailed, and blue-throated hummingbirds. Hummingbirds sometimes follow woodpeckers called sapsuckers around the forest to get sap from the holes they drill.

Many people put out hummingbird feeders, filled with sugar water to attract hummingbirds. But sometimes they attract other animals:

- Sphinx moths, which are often mistaken for hummingbirds, may drink from hummingbird feeders in the evening.
- Orioles, which are large birds, may pull apart a hummingbird feeder to drink the sugar water inside.
- Bats visit feeders in southeast Arizona. Some bat species specialize in drinking nectar from flowers at night. So hummingbird feeders are perfect for them.
- Bears visit hummingbird feeders in some wild areas. Unfortunately, the bears usually pull apart the feeder in order to get to the sugar water. So people in bear areas sometimes bring their hummingbird feeders indoors at night.

# Attracting Hummingbirds

Planting flowers that provide hummingbirds with nectar is one of the best ways to attract these birds. Contact a local nature center or garden center for native plants that grow well in your area.

Hummingbird feeders work well, too. But you have to keep the feeders clean. Otherwise, you harm the birds more than you help them.

A good hummingbird feeder has red parts, to attract the birds. Do not add red food coloring to the nectar. Some scientists think this food coloring harms the birds. To make nectar, get an adult's help. Mix four parts water with one part sugar. Boil this mixture two minutes, then let it cool. Pour it in the feeders. Never use honey or artificial sweeteners in feeders.

Clean the feeder once or twice a week, with a solution of one part bleach to ten parts water. Use a bottle brush to get out any mold. Rinse the feeder thoroughly with water. Then fill it with the sugar-water solution, and put it outside again.

Then you can enjoy nature's fast-flying acrobats, the amazing hummingbirds!

For more information on hummingbirds, check these sources:

Sayre, April Pulley. "Hummingbirds." *Ranger Rick*, August 1998, pp. 18–25.

Sayre, Jeff, and April Sayre. *Hummingbirds: the Sun Catchers*. Minnetonka, MN: NorthWord Press, 1996.

Stokes, Donald, and Lillian Stokes. *The Hummingbird Book*. Boston: Little, Brown, and Co., 1989.

April Pulley Sayre's Web site: www.aprilsayre.com

Southeast Arizona Bird Observatory: www.sabo.org

Hummingbirds! Web site by Lenny Chambers: www.hummingbirds.net

*For my grandmother, Pearl Harlow Richardson.*

*Many thanks to my husband, Jeff Sayre, for his help on this book. Thank you also to Sherri Williamson of the Southeast Arizona Bird Observatory.*

—A. P. H.


*To my mother, Martha Righter Willman.*
—G. W. H.

Published by:
The Millbrook Press, Inc.
2 Old New Milford Road
Brookfield, Connecticut 06804
www.millbrookpress.com

Library of Congress Cataloging-in-Publication Data
Sayre, April Pulley.
The hungry hummingbird / by April Pulley Sayre; illustrated by Gay W. Holland.
p. cm.
ISBN 0-7613-1951-4 (lib. bdg.)
1. Hummingbirds—Food—Juvenile literature. [Hummingbirds. 2. Birds—Habits
and behavior.] I. Holland, Gay W. II. Title.
QL696.A558 S274 2001
598.7'64—dc21    00-050064

Printed in Hong Kong
5  4  3  2  1